GOLDEN STATE
WARRIORS

TOM PETERSON

CREATIVE EDUCATION

Photo Credit: Creative Education would like to thank NBA photographer Ron Koch (New York City) for the color photography in this series.

Published by Creative Education Inc., 123 South Broad Street, Mankato, Minnesota 56001.

ISBN: 0-88682-204-1

In 1839, German immigrant John Augustus Sutter founded a colony in Mexican territory along the Sacramento River. This site would later be known as Sacramento, California. In 1848, gold was discovered at Sutter's sawmill. The gold rush had begun. Thousands of people poured into California to seek their fortune panning for gold.

The gold rush brought instant prosperity and fame to the region. Little wonder, then, that California is commonly known as the Golden State. And it seems only fitting that one of the area's most popular professional basketball teams is named the Golden State Warriors.

The Warriors, one of the NBA's most enduring teams, have given professional basketball an impressive string of Hall-of-Famers. Such legendary figures as Joe Fulks, Eddie Gottlieb, Tom Gola, Wilt Chamberlain, Al Attles and Rick Barry have proudly played or coached for the club over the years.

The Warriors' tradition goes back all the way to the beginnings of pro basketball in the United States. The year was 1946. World War II was finally over, and Americans were in a mood to celebrate and have fun. Big league baseball and football games had already gained loyal followings, and now pro basketball was about to explode in popularity.

The National Basketball Association would not be established until 1949. Meanwhile, the NBA's predecessor, the Basketball Association of America, debuted in 1946 with nine teams, including the Philadelphia Warriors.

Philadelphia's star player was Joe Fulks, a skinny 6-foot-5 Kentuckian who had enlisted in the Marine Corps right out of Murray State College. After fighting in the battles of Guam and Iwo Jima, Fulks got his discharge and signed up for the BAA's inaugural season, 1946-47. He became the league's first star and scoring champion.

With Fulks being fed by Philadelphia's outstanding guard and playmaker Howie Dallmar, the Warriors streaked to the first ever BAA title, beating Chicago 83-80 in the sixth game of the championship series. For their efforts, the Philadelphia players each received a $2,000 bonus, an amount equal to their entire annual salary.

The Warriors had fallen out of contention by the early 1950s, finishing dead-last in their division. But by the 1955-56 season, under new coach George Senesky, the club was ready to make another drive for the league championship.

Joe Barry Carroll puts up a shot over the arms of New York Knicks defender Bill Cartwright.

In a single season, Senesky transformed the
Warriors into the highest scoring team in NBA
history. The team's chief weapons were Paul
Arizin and Neil Johnston who combined for 46
points per game, but there were others as well.

Flanking Johnston and Arizin, the Warriors
had Joe Graboske and Walt Davis to provide
strong rebounding. Their prize rookie, Tom Gola,
was a full-fledged back court man who stood
nearly 6-foot-6. Jack George, Ernie Beck and
George Dempsey filled out a versatile set of
guards. In the '56 playoffs, the Warriors got off to
a fine start and never looked back, beating the
Celtics by six games, and then knocking off the
Syracuse Nats and the Fort Wayne Pistons.

The Warriors of 1955-56 were the last team to
hold the NBA title before Red Auerbach's Boston Celtics began their amazing 13-year dynasty.
Coming out of college the next year to join the
Celtics was the one-and-only Bill Russell, a 6-
foot-9 center with extraordinary defensive skills.

Russell's league-wide superiority at center
would go unchallenged until the Warriors drafted
a 7-foot-2, 300-pound giant named Wilton Nor-
man Chamberlain.

Born and raised in Philadelphia, Wilt drew national attention for his height and skill during his
senior year at Overbrook High School. Hundreds
of scholarship offers poured in from colleges and
universities across the land. Wilt, however, chose
the University of Kansas because of its long and
storied basketball tradition.

■

*Paul Arizin (11) and Bob Cousy of the Boston Celtics
go after a loose ball in a 1960 NBA playoff game.*

As an NBA rookie, Chamberlain easily won the scoring title with an incredible 37.6 points per game average. He also out-rebounded everyone in the league, including Bill Russell, as he led the Warriors to a 49-26 season, the best record in the history of the club. Unfortunately for the Warriors, the Celtics finished at 59-16 and went on to win their second straight NBA championship.

For his first three seasons in the league, Chamberlain was such a dominant offensive player that he simply made a mockery of all previous NBA scoring records.

During the 1961-62 season, Chamberlain had a year that staggers the imagination. He averaged 50.4 points per game, including the famous March 2, 1962, assault on the New York Knicks in which he scored an all-time NBA high 100 points in a single game. Despite Chamberlain's scoring, the Warriors still came up 11 wins short of the Celtics in the Eastern Division that year, and the NBA players again chose Bill Russell over Chamberlain in the MVP voting.

Meanwhile, the Warriors' fans were becoming increasingly disenchanted. They had been counting on Chamberlain to single-handedly deliver the NBA title. Slowly but steadily, the crowds at Convention Hall were dwindling to the danger point. Even Chamberlain's historic 100-point game drew only 4,000 Philadelphia

Wilt Chamberlain

After 16 years in the City of Brotherly Love, the Warriors were moving to the City by the Bay.

fans. It came as no real surprise, then, when the Warriors' front office began shopping around for a new home.

Just prior to the 1962-63 season, owner Eddie Gottlieb publicly confirmed his decision to sell the team to a San Francisco group. After 16 years in the City of Brotherly Love, the Warriors were moving to the City by the Bay in hopes of finding a bigger, more loyal following.

Joe Fulks

The move didn't really improve things for the Warriors. In the Warriors' first home game in San Francisco's famous Cow Palace, Chamberlain rammed through his customary 56 points, but only 5,000 San Franciscans showed up that night to welcome the team to town. Once again, Chamberlain went on to win the NBA scoring title, his fourth straight. And once again, the Warriors ended the season with a disappointing record, this time sinking all the way to 31-49.

Chamberlain was stuck in the middle of a confusing dilemma. Simultaneously, he was considered to be the Warriors' greatest asset and their worst liability. No one seemed to be able to solve the riddle. If Wilt scored 50 points a game, he was considered a ball hog or a one dimensional player. But if he didn't score 50 points, the fans went home disappointed.

In the 1963-64 season, new Warriors' coach Alex Hannum offered a simple solution to the problem. "For us to

Simultaneously, he was considered to be the Warriors' greatest asset and their worst liability.

win," said Hannum, "Wilt had to play like Bill Russell on one end of the court and like Wilt Chamberlain at the other end of the court. Russell is the greatest defensive player in the league, and Wilt is the greatest offensive player. The new Chamberlain will have to combine the best of both."

The giants meet: Archrivals Wilt Chamberlain (13) and Bill Russell (6) go head-to-head in a thriller between the Warriors and the Celtics.

Under Hannum's rule, forwards Tom Meschery and Wayne Hightower, backed up by exciting, 6-foot-11 rookie Nate Thurmond, assumed more of the scoring burden, freeing Chamberlain to become a menacing defender. The strategy worked. Wilt still led the league in scoring, but his average dropped eight points while the Warriors' victory total increased by 17, enough to claim the Western Division title.

"We have become the best defensive team in the league," Coach Hannum said after the final regular season game, "but we couldn't have done it without Al." Hannum, who was selected 1963-64 Coach of the Year, was referring to unheralded Al Attles, the short, stocky guard who had snuck in the Warriors' back door as a fifth-round draft choice out of North Carolina back in 1960.

At 6 feet tall, 195 pounds, Attles was built like a wrecking ball. A fierce competitor who averaged 10 points a game, Attles specialized in rugged, ball-hawking defense. And while Chamberlain may have been able to benchpress 400 pounds, it was burly little Al Attles who served as the Warriors' enforcer. In a game against St. Louis, for example, Warrior Tom Meschery was knocked down by a punch from Zelmo Beaty, the Hawks' massive, 6-foot-9 center. Instantly, Attles came to the rescue, bowling Beaty all the way into the stands with a shoulder charge.

Nate "The Great" Thurmond (42) muscles a rebound against the 76ers.

The new look Warriors marched all the way to the 1964 world championship series where they were matched against the Celtics. Suddenly, the entire San Francisco Bay Area was filled with excitement. Would this be the year that the Warriors finally toppled the Celtic dynasty?

Back in Boston, Celtic center Bill Russell received special orders from Red Auerbach. Russell was to force Chamberlain away from the basket so that Wilt would have to rely on his secondary fallaway shot, rather than his sure-fire dunk. If the shot missed, Chamberlain would be left out of position for the rebound.

Auerbach's strategy paid off, as the Celtics won yet another league championship. Losing that particular series was a terrible blow for the Warriors and their fans. When the next season found the Warriors getting off to

the worst start in franchise history, coach Hannum summed up the situation. "We have the talent to win it all, but for some reason we can't seem to get our attitude on track," he said.

By mid-season, the same team that had nearly snatched the NBA title just a few months earlier was now the league's most lackluster club. Even the spirited play of Al Attles did little to inspire his listless teammates. Trade rumors ran rampant as the team searched for a way to get back on track.

Finally, the rumors were confirmed. The Warriors had traded the great Wilt Chamberlain back to Philadelphia for $300,000 and three undistinguished players.

In one bold stroke, owner Frank Mieuli had dealt away his biggest star, but also unloaded Chamberlain's huge paycheck, about one-third of the team's total payroll. Although Chamberlain was gone, a bright new chapter in the Warriors' story was about to begin.

The Warriors had traded the great Wilt Chamberlain back to Philadelphia for $300,000 and three undistinguished players.

After finishing the 1964-65 season at 17-63, the worst record in the entire NBA, the Warriors used its top draft pick to acquire Rick Barry. A rail thin University of Miami forward, Barry soon became one of the NBA's all-time great shooters.

On a good night, Barry could score from 25 feet out. In addition, his unusual between-the-knees freethrow style proved to be the most accurate in the league. Though his teammates worried about the frail looking 22-year-old, Barry held his own against the toughest NBA forwards and eventually earned Rookie of the Year honors by averaging 25.7 points a game. As a result, the Warriors notched twice the number of wins as the year before.

Meanwhile, Nate Thurmond was developing into a first rate center even though the San Francisco media rarely gave him the credit he deserved. "I guess you've got to have some kind of flair and I don't," said Thurmond, a player who quietly did his job, and did it well. "About the only fancy thing I do is block a few shots every game," he added modestly.

Unfortunately, the NBA kept no statistics on blocked shots during Thurmond's era. No one will ever really know just how many balls were batted down by his long, sinewy arms. "I lost count after Nate rejected six shots by the middle of the third quarter against the Lakers one night," said former Celtic star Bill Sharman who coached the Warriors from 1966-68. Clearly, Thurmond's defense and Rick Barry's offense were the keys to the Warriors' rebuilding program.

■

On a good night Rick Barry could score at will from almost anywhere on the court.

By the end of the 1966-67 season, Barry had captured the league scoring title, snapping Chamberlain's string of seven straight. In the playoffs, the Warriors rolled over Los Angeles and St. Louis to become the Western Division champs. Next they faced the Philadelphia 76ers, led by their old teammate Wilt Chamberlain in the NBA Finals.

Although Barry averaged an amazing 41 points per game during the series, the 76ers prevailed. In the sixth and deciding game, Chamberlain and Wally Jones led a magnificent fourth period comeback to defeat the Warriors by three points.

Naturally, the Warriors' fans had high hopes for the following season, but two events combined to spoil their chances for a championship season. First, Barry jumped ship to the rival American Basketball Association in order to play for the Oakland Oaks, a

Chamberlain and Wally Jones led a magnificent fourth period comeback . . .

Rick Barry

team coached by Barry's father-in-law. Then, halfway through the season, Nate Thurmond was sidelined with an injury. Without their stars, the team slumped to third place in their division.

Neither Coach Sharman nor his replacement George Lee could turn the Warriors' fortunes around over the next two seasons. With 30 games left in the 1969-70 campaign, a new era began when Al Attles succeeded Lee to become the tenth head coach in the history of the franchise.

Attles would have preferred to continue just as a player, but he finally agreed to be a player/coach for two seasons "just to help the team." As it turned out, Attles would "help the team" for the next twelve years, an era that included eight straight winning seasons and one world championship.

Off the court, Attles was very active in pushing for a permanent home for the Warriors, who had split their home games between Oakland, San Jose and San Francisco since 1962. In 1971, the club moved to the Oakland Coliseum and renamed itself the Golden State Warriors.

Jeff Mullin

On the court, Coach Attles was an innovator. He experimented with dozens of starting lineups during his first three seasons. In an effort to fill Barry's shoes at forward, Attles rotated Jerry Lucas, Clyde Lee and Cazzie Russell.

In the back court, Attles was forever looking for a second guard to run with Jeff Mullins, a steady veteran who usually managed to score 20 points, grab five rebounds and dish out five assists a game.

For three straight seasons under Attles, the Warriors staged an exciting showdown with the Milwaukee Bucks in the Western Conference semifinals, but each year would fall a bit short.

Meanwhile, the Warriors' front office never stopped trying to get Rick Barry back. It was said that owner Frank Mieuli even had Barry's No. 24 hanging in his office. Eventually, Barry did return to the NBA, and was back in a Warriors uniform for the 1973-74 season.

It was said that Warriors owner Frank Mieuli even had Barry's No. 24 hanging in his office.

■
Al Attles took the helm in the 1969-70 campaign, becoming the tenth head coach in the history of the franchise.

When the 1974-75 season began with Barry as the only returning starter, the Warriors were expected to finish last in their division. Coach Attles revamped his lineup, moving third year guard Charles Johnson into the back court with journeyman Butch Beard. Mullins came off the bench along with rookie Phil Smith and the unknown Charlie Dudley. Starting at forward was Jamaal Wilkes from UCLA. Rookie Derrek Dickey and veteran boardman Bill Bridges provided relief. At center, former Chicago Bulls reserve Clifford Ray alternated with 6-foot-11 George Johnson.

It was a strange but determined team. Their style was marked by nonstop running and aggressive, gambling defense. Barry was the key, leading his team in scoring, assists, foul shooting and minutes played. But Attles' strategy called for every single player, including the bench, to contribute. Teams with only seven or eight good players simply could not keep up with the ever rotating Warriors, especially as the game wore on.

It was a strange but determined team, marked by nonstop running and aggressive, gambling defense.

Together, the Warriors swept to the Pacific Division championship. In the playoffs, they stunned Chicago in seven games, winning the deciding contest on the Bulls' home court. Next came the world championship match-up with K.C. Jones' powerful Washington Bullets. The Bullets were heavily favored, but the Warriors were undaunted. By maintaining the same level of poise and team balance that had carried them into the playoffs, the Warriors won the NBA championship in grand fashion, with a four game sweep of the Bullets.

Power up front: The Warriors relied upon the strong rebounding of 6-foot-11 George Johnson in the mid-1970s.

No one was more surprised than Rick Barry. "We made reality out of fantasy," said Barry, the series' Most Valuable Player. "Even when we fell 8 points behind at the end (of the final game), our whole bench was saying, 'we're going to win this' 8 down, in a road game. You figure it out. This is one gutsy group of guys."

With Barry and 6-foot-4 swingman Phil Smith leading the way, Golden State again topped the Western Division the following season. But their game soured in the seventh and deciding game of the conference finals against Phoenix. It was the first sign of a gradual decline that would see the Warriors sink lower in the standings over the next few years.

By the 1977-78 season, more than half the players from the championship club had been cut, traded or retired. Barry himself left Golden State the next season, playing one more year in the league before retiring.

But there was plenty of reason for optimism, even though the Warriors missed the playoffs both in 1980-81 and 1981-82. On hot nights the Warriors rode the scoring of Bernard King, 23.2 points per game average; World B. Free, 22.9; Joe Barry Carroll, 17.0; and the dangerous Purvis Short, 14.4.

Unfortunately, the Warriors began the very next season by losing free agent King to New York. From there, the story only got worse, as virtually the entire team was sidelined due to injury or illness.

After averaging 23.2 points per game in the 1981-82 season, Bernard King became a free agent and signed with New York.

At the end of the season, coach Attles moved up to become the club's general manager, and John Bach took over as coach. Bach proved to be a sincere, hard working man with a good mind for the game, but his Warriors still lost 174 games from 1983 to 1986. This record was a direct result, said most experts, of owner Franklin Mieuli's temperamental leadership.

Not only did the team have an inexperienced coach, but they were also left without any first round draft picks in 1984. When Golden State finished the next two seasons with disastrous records, it was clear the team was in need of a new direction.

In 1986, James Fitzgerald and Daniel Finnane became the new owners of the Warriors and installed George Karl as head coach.

Karl, fresh from a successful stint as head coach of the Cleveland Cavaliers, proceeded to turn the club around. In his first season as coach, 1986-87, the team improved its record by 12 games over the previous year. More importantly, the Warriors also advanced to the semifinal round of the playoffs. It was the team's first playoff appearance in ten years.

■

Warrior on the move: Golden State's high scoring Purvis Short (left) drives past Seattle's Lonnie Shelton.

Leading the way for the Warriors that season were the club's NBA All-Star game representatives, Joe Barry Carroll and Eric "Sleepy" Floyd.

Carroll, an All-American out of Purdue, was the Warriors' first pick in the 1980 college draft. He was also the number one pick overall. By the 1986-87 season, Carroll had become one of the league's premier centers, leading the Warriors not only in scoring, averaging over 21 points a game, but also in blocked shots with 123.

Floyd established himself as a topflight point guard by making over 800 assists that year. This mark broke a 21-year old club record, and placed him second in the league. He also set a Warrior record for 3-point field goals with 73.

Despite their success in 1986-87, the Warriors got off to a dreadful 3-15 start the next season. In an effort to make a new beginning, the Warriors traded their two All-Stars, Carroll and Floyd, for 7-foot-4 center Ralph Sampson from the Houston Rockets.

The Warriors looked to Sampson, a four time All-Star

. . .observers believed Sampson had not always fulfilled his potential, but the Warriors had confidence. . .

game representative, to spark the club. While some NBA observers believed Sampson had not always fulfilled his potential, the Warriors had confidence he would succeed in his role.

"He has to dominate as an all-around player," said general manager Don Nelson. "He would fail if we wanted him to score 30 (points) and get 16 rebounds

Towering Ralph Sampson was obtained from Houston during 1987-88 in exchange for All-Stars Joe Barry Carroll and Eric Floyd.

every night. But he can do a good job with those things and with his passing, his ball handling and his shotblocking. He is, in fact, the modern-day center because he's so versatile."

Indeed, Sampson played well for the Warriors, averaging over 15 points per game, while improving his overall style of play.

While the faces were changing on the court, changes were being made behind the bench as well. Coach Karl did not always see eye to eye with Nelson, who had been an outstanding coach for the Milwaukee Bucks before taking his front office job with the Warriors. Before the end of the season, Karl had resigned, setting the stage for Nelson to take over as head coach the following season.

The juggling of coaches, combined with numerous roster changes, made for a tumultuous season. To add to the team's problems, Sampson suffered an injury that kept him out of the lineup for the last two months of the season. The Warriors also missed the play of guard Chris Mullin, who spent part of the season in an alcohol rehabilitation center, but returned to lead the club in total points. He also had the team's highest scoring average with 20.2 points per game. Unfortunately, it was not enough to boost the team into the playoffs.

However, the dismal season failed to deter the team. Having gone through a rebuilding period, the club seemed only a player or two away from being a playoff contender. With Nelson, a two time NBA Coach of the Year, guiding the team, the Warriors had high expectations. With any luck, the future will return a second gold rush of success to the Warriors. But there is no doubt that the Golden State Warriors will continue to entertain and delight their fans in their quest for the NBA title.

■